Orca Calves

by Ruth Owen

Consultant:
Dr. David Lusseau
MASTS Senior Lecturer in Marine Top Predator Biology
University of Aberdeen
School of Biological Sciences
Aberdeen, Scotland

BEARPORT
PUBLISHING
New York, New York

Credits

Cover, © Minden Pictures/SuperStock; 4–5, ©Flip Nicklin/Minden Pictures/FLPA; 6, ©Cosmographics; 7, ©Miles Away Photography/Shutterstock; 8–9, ©Norbert Wu/Minden Pictures/FLPA; 9C, ©Kelly Funk/All Canada Photos/Superstock; 11, ©Amos Nachoum/Corbis and ©Gerard Lacz/age fotostock/Superstock; 12–13, ©Gerard Lacz/Animals Animals; 14–15, ©Suzi Eszterhas/Minden Pictures/FLPA; 16–17, ©Kathryn Jeffs/Nature Picture Library and ©David Pruter/Shutterstock; 19T, ©Doug Allan/Nature Picture Library; 19B, ©Kathryn Jeffs/Nature Picture Library; 20–21, ©Gerard Lacz/age fotostock/Superstock; 22T, ©Kelly Funk/All Canada Photos/Superstock; 22C, ©Hiroya Minakuchi/FLPA; 22B, ©Miles Away Photography/Shutterstock; 23T, ©KKulikov/Shutterstock; 23C, ©Monika Wieland/Shutterstock; 23B, ©Xavier Marchant/Shutterstock.

Publisher: Kenn Goin
Senior Editor: Lisa Wiseman
Creative Director: Spencer Brinker
Design: Emma Randall
Editor: Mark J Sachner
Photo Researcher: Ruby Tuesday Books Ltd

Library of Congress Cataloging-in-Publication Data

Owen, Ruth, 1967–
  Orca calves / Ruth Owen.
    p. cm. — (Water babies)
  Includes bibliographical references and index.
  ISBN 978-1-61772-600-2 (library binding) — ISBN 1-61772-600-1 (library binding)
  1. Killer whale—Infancy—Juvenile literature. I. Title.
  QL737.C432O946 2013
  599.53'61392—dc23
                              2012012880

For more information, write to Bearport Publishing Company, Inc., 45 West 21st Street, Suite 3B, New York, New York 10010. Printed in the United States of America.

10 9 8 7 6 5 4 3 2 1

Contents

Meet an orca calf

Out in the ocean, three pointed, black **fins** appear from under the water.

fin

adult orca

The fins belong to three adult orcas.

Suddenly, an orca **calf** leaps from the water and splashes back down again.

It is having fun swimming with its family.

orca calf

All about orcas

Orcas are a type of **whale**.

They live in oceans all over the world.

Adult orcas can be as long as eight children lying head to toe in a line.

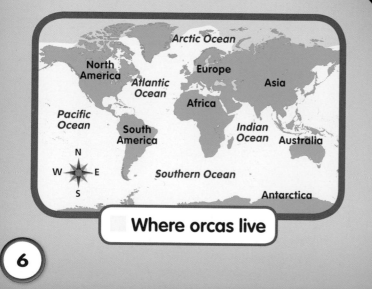

Arctic Ocean

North America

Europe

Atlantic Ocean

Asia

Africa

Pacific Ocean

South America

Indian Ocean

Australia

N
W   E
S

Southern Ocean

Antarctica

Where orcas live

An adult male orca may have a fin that is taller than an adult human.

fin

adult orca

Adult orca size

Ocean mammals

Orcas may look a little like huge **fish**, but they are **mammals**.

Like all mammals, orcas need air to breathe.

They cannot breathe underwater, as fish do.

Instead, they swim to the surface to breathe in air.

An orca breathes through a **blowhole** on top of its head.

blowhole

A calf is born

Like other mammals, orcas give birth to live babies.

A mother orca gives birth to her calf underwater.

As soon as the baby orca leaves its mother's body, it begins to swim.

The mother and calf swim to the water's surface.

Then the little orca uses its blowhole to take its first breath of air.

newborn calf

mother

mother

orca calf

Feeding on the move

An orca drinks milk from its mother's body until it is two or three years old.

The mother and calf don't stop moving when it's feeding time.

Together they move slowly through the water while the calf feeds.

mother orca

calf feeding

An orca family

An orca calf lives with its mother in a family group.

The group might include the calf's older brothers, sisters, aunts, uncles, and grandmother.

mother orca

A calf's father is a member of a different family group.

He doesn't live with the calf or help care for it.

orca family

orca calf

Orca food

Orcas eat seals, sea lions, dolphins, and other types of whales.

They also eat sharks, other fish, sea turtles, and seabirds.

An orca calf may begin to eat some fish when it is about one year old.

seal

Hunting skills

The mother orca and older family members teach a calf how to hunt.

Sometimes the orcas hunt as a team.

In cold oceans, seals rest on floating chunks of ice.

The orcas swim toward the ice to make a big wave.

The wave washes the seal into the water so the orcas can catch it!

seal

adult orca

calf

wave

19

Family life

An orca stays with its family for its whole life.

It becomes an adult when it is about ten years old.

A young female learns how to care for calves by watching older mothers.

Finally, when she is about 15 years old, she is ready to have a calf of her own!

Glossary

blowhole (BLOH-hohl) the opening on the top of a whale's head that allows the animal to take in and let out air

calf (KAF) the baby of an animal such as a whale or a manatee

fins (FINZ) pointed body parts on the backs of ocean animals such as orcas, dolphins, and sharks

fish (FISH) cold-blooded animals that mostly have young by laying eggs

mammals (MAM-uhlz) warm-blooded animals that usually have fur or hair; most mammals give birth to live babies and feed them milk from their bodies

whale (WALE) a large mammal that lives in the ocean

Index

Read more

Harris, Caroline. *Whales and Dolphins (Discover Science).* Boston: Kingfisher (2010).

Lunis, Natalie. *Killer Whale: The World's Largest Dolphin (More SuperSized!).* New York: Bearport Publishing (2010).

Oldfield, Dawn Bluemel. *Killer Whale: Water Bullet! (Blink of an Eye: Superfast Animals).* New York: Bearport Publishing (2011).

Learn more online

To learn more about orcas, visit
www.bearportpublishing.com/WaterBabies

About the author

Ruth Owen has been writing children's books for more than ten years. She particularly enjoys working on books about animals and the natural world. Ruth lives in Cornwall, England, just minutes from the ocean. She loves gardening and caring for her family of llamas.